MW01098830

Capstone 09 18.99

Land of Liberty

Washington

by **Kim Covert**

Consultant:
Kelly Billington
Board Member
Washington State Council for
Social Studies

Capstone
press
Mankato, Minnesota

Capstone Press
151 Good Counsel Drive • P.O. Box 669 • Mankato, Minnesota 56002
http://www.capstone-press.com

Library of Congress Cataloging-in-Publication Data
Covert, Kim.
  Washington/by Kim Covert.
    p. cm.—(Land of liberty)
  Includes bibliographical references and index.
  ISBN 0-7368-2203-8
  Contents: About Washington—Land, climate, and wildlife—History of
Washington—Government and politics—Economy and resources—People and
culture.
    1. Washington (State)—Juvenile literature. [1. Washington (State)]
I. Title. II. Series.
F891.3.C68 2004
979.7—dc21   2002155827

Summary: An introduction to the geography, history, government, politics,
    economy, resources, people, and culture of Washington, including maps,
    charts, and a recipe.

Editorial Credits
Rebecca Glaser, editor; Jennifer Schonborn, series designer; Linda Clavel, book
    designer; Enoch Peterson, illustrator; Jo Miller, photo researcher; Eric Kudalis,
    product planning editor

Photo Credits
Cover images: Meadows by the Cascades, Corbis; Seattle skyline, Digital Stock

Capstone Press/Gary Sundermeyer, 54; Corbis/Reuters NewMedia Inc., 35; David
Jensen, 8, 12–13; Digital Vision Ltd., 1; Gary Braasch, 4; Gnass Photo Images/Jon
Gnass, 38; Houserstock, 32; Houserstock/Dave G. Houser, 42; Microsoft, 41;
MSCUA/ University of Washington Libraries, 18, 21, 22–23, 24, 27, 58; One
Mile Up Inc., 55 (both); Oscar C. Williams, 31; PhotoDisc, Inc., 57; Photri-
Microstock, 29; Tom & Pat Leeson, 15, 16, 17, 44–45, 56, 63; U.S. Postal
Service, 59; The Viesti Collection Inc./Alan Kearney, 52–53; Wolfgang
Kaehler/www.kaehlerphoto.com, 46, 50

Artistic Effects
Brand X Pictures, Corbis, Image Ideas Inc., PhotoDisc Inc.

1 2 3 4 5 6 08 07 06 05 04 03

Table of Contents

Clouds of ash filled the sky around Mount St. Helens when it erupted in 1980.

Chapter 1

About Washington

On May 18, 1980, a volcanic eruption blasted huge clouds of hot ash into the sky. The north side of Mount St. Helens broke off and slid downward. A landslide of mud, rock, and ice slid into Spirit Lake. The mass then roared 14 miles (23 kilometers) down the Toutle River. The eruption lasted nine hours. It destroyed about 1,300 feet (400 meters) of the volcano. Winds carried volcanic ash all the way to the eastern border of Washington.

The Mount St. Helens eruption harmed wildlife, land, and people. Millions of deer, elk, bears, and birds were killed. About 230 square miles (600 square kilometers) of forest were destroyed. Fifty-seven people died. Many buildings, bridges,

roads, and machines were also destroyed. The volcano caused losses of more than $1.8 billion in crops and property.

Despite the great amount of damage, the area has recovered. Plants are growing there again. More than 10 million trees were planted to replace lost forests. Elk and black-tailed deer have returned.

In 1982, the Mount St. Helens National Volcanic Monument was established. Scientists there observe how the environment responds to the disaster. Visitor centers present information about the effects of the eruption.

The Evergreen State

Washington is famous for its natural beauty. It has snow-covered mountains, rolling hills, and beautiful coastal waters. It is nicknamed the Evergreen State for its thick, green forests. Washington has the largest amount of forested land in the United States.

Washington lies on the Pacific Coast in the northwestern part of the country. Only two U.S. states border Washington. Idaho lies to its east. Oregon is to the south. The state lies to the south of British Columbia, Canada. The Pacific Ocean forms the state's western border.

Washington Cities

CANADA

BRITISH COLUMBIA

Strait of Georgia

Strait of Juan de Fuca

● Bellingham

— *Puget Sound*

PACIFIC OCEAN

Bremerton ●

Seattle
● ● Bellevue

Tacoma ●

Olympia ✪

Columbia River

WASHINGTON

Spokane ●

IDAHO

Yakima ●

Snake River

Kennewick ●

● Walla Walla

● Vancouver

Columbia River

OREGON

Legend

▢	American Indian Reservation
✪	Capital
●	City
～	River

N
W — E
S

Scale

Miles

0	30	60	90

0	30	60	90	120

Kilometers

Mount Rainier in the Cascades is the highest point in Washington.

Chapter 2

Land, Climate, and Wildlife

Natural land features create five regions in Washington. The Olympic Mountains and Puget Sound Lowlands lie near the Pacific Ocean. The Cascade Range divides the state in half. The Columbia Plateau and the Rocky Mountains make up the eastern part of Washington.

Pacific Regions

Washington's Olympic Mountains region lies on a peninsula that reaches into the Pacific Ocean. The mountains rise from a temperate rain forest that is just above sea level. The largest western hemlocks, red cedars, and noble firs in the nation grow there. A national park protects part of the Olympic Mountains and rain forest.

The other coastal region is the Puget Sound Lowlands. This region surrounds Puget Sound and extends south. Puget Sound is a long, narrow ocean bay with more than 300 islands. Major ports and cities lie along the shores of the sound. More people live in this area than in any other part of Washington.

The Cascade Range

The snowcapped Cascade Range stretches from Canada into northern California. Crossing through west-central Washington, the Cascades split the state.

Mount Rainier, the highest point in the state, is in the Cascades. It stands 14,410 feet (4,392 meters) above sea level. Mount St. Helens is also in this region.

Washington's Land Features

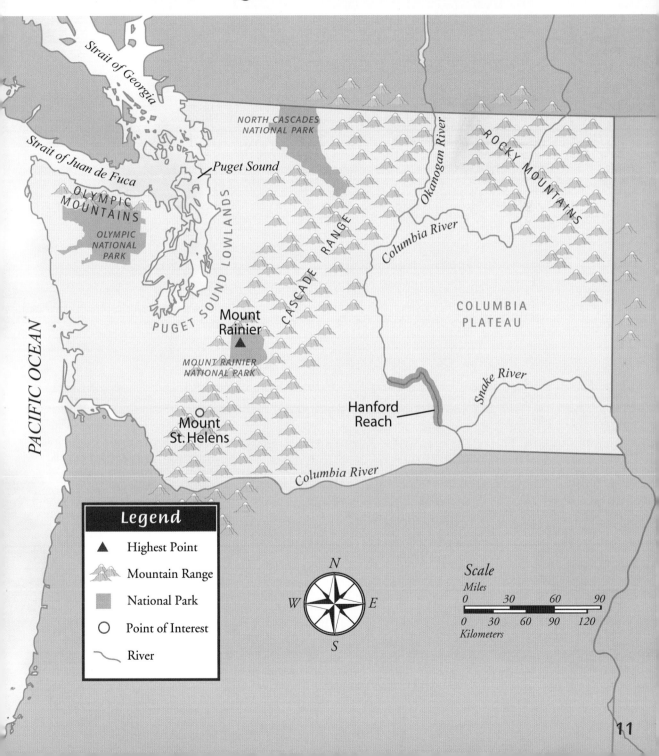

Strait of Georgia

Strait of Juan de Fuca

NORTH CASCADES
NATIONAL PARK

Puget Sound

OLYMPIC
MOUNTAINS

OLYMPIC
NATIONAL
PARK

Okanogan River

ROCKY MOUNTAINS

Columbia River

PUGET SOUND LOWLANDS

CASCADE RANGE

PACIFIC OCEAN

COLUMBIA
PLATEAU

Mount
Rainier

▲

MOUNT RAINIER
NATIONAL PARK

Snake River

Mount
St. Helens

○

Hanford
Reach

Columbia River

Legend

▲ Highest Point

🏔 Mountain Range

■ National Park

○ Point of Interest

〰 River

N
W E
S

Scale
Miles
0   30   60   90
0   30   60   90   120
Kilometers

11

The Columbia Plateau

The Columbia Plateau stretches across eastern Washington. A rim of mountains surrounds this low area. The Columbia Plateau is part of the largest lava plateau in the world. Thousands of years ago, lava flowed out the earth's crust.

The Columbia River is one of the longest rivers in the United States. It flows through the state for more than 700 miles (1,100 kilometers). In southern Washington, it turns west and empties into the Pacific Ocean.

The Rocky Mountains

The northern Rocky Mountains cut across the northeastern corner of Washington. Most of these mountains are between 3,000 and 7,000 feet (900 to 2,100 meters) high. Forests cover most of the mountains. The Columbia and the Okanogan are the main rivers in the region. Minerals found in this area include clay, copper, gold, lead, limestone, silver, and zinc.

The Columbia River separates southern Washington and northern Oregon.

> *"The serenity of the climate, the innumerable pleasing landscapes, and the abundant fertility that unassisted nature puts forth, require only . . . the industry of man . . . to render it the most lovely country that can be imagined."*
>
> *–George Vancouver, 1792 at Puget Sound*

Climate

The Pacific Ocean and the Cascade Range affect Washington's climate. Wet winds from the Pacific give the area west of the Cascades mild, rainy winters and cool summers.

The Cascades stop moisture from moving east. Clouds drop their rain west of the mountains, creating a drier climate east of the Cascades. In the western city of Seattle, the average precipitation is 37 inches (94 centimeters) per year. In the eastern town of Spokane, it is only 17 inches (43 centimeters) per year. Much of the Yakima Valley in south-central Washington is semidesert. It receives less than 8 inches (20 centimeters) of rain annually. The Columbia Plateau receives little rain. Farmers irrigate the land. They use equipment to bring water to their crops.

Wildlife

The wilderness areas of Washington provide homes for many animals. Deer, bears, mountain goats, and coyotes are among

Farmlands cover much of eastern Washington.

the mammals. Coastal waters are home to whales, sea lions, and seals. Birds found in Washington's forests include bald eagles, hawks, and owls. Great blue herons and loons catch fish in inland waters.

Fish live in Washington's freshwater and ocean areas. Five types of Pacific salmon swim up the Columbia River to spawn, or lay eggs.

Environmental Issues

The Hanford Reach is an area of the Columbia River where Chinook salmon spawn. Some people want to build dams on the river. Salmon cannot easily swim upstream to spawn when dams block their way. For years, some of Washington's

Salmon swim up the Columbia River each year to spawn, or lay eggs.

Northern Spotted Owl

Since 1991, the northern spotted owl has been an endangered species. Spotted owls live in Washington's older forests. Loggers have cut down forests where the spotted owls live.

Each pair of owls needs 100 acres (40 hectares) of forest for nesting and hunting. They may nest in the tops of broken trees or in holes in the tree trunks.

Laws banning the cutting of older forests caused the lumber industry to lose money. Today, the state is looking for ways to protect the spotted owl without hurting the lumber industry.

lawmakers have been trying to pass laws to protect Hanford Reach. They want to protect the salmon in the river.

In 2002, the state had 48 hazardous waste sites that needed to be cleaned up. These areas contain materials no longer used by factories. The waste sites can be dangerous to people, animals, and the environment. Washingtonians are working on ways to reduce waste and pollution.

Animals and faces are the subjects of rock art drawn long ago by the Makah Indians in northwestern Washington.

Chapter 3

History of Washington

About 12,000 years ago, ancient peoples lived in the Washington area. Ancestors of today's American Indians lived there by the 1500s.

The Nooksak, Chinook, Nisqually, Clallam, Makah, Quinault, and Puyallup tribes lived along the coast. These western groups built longhouses near the ocean or along a river. Fish was a main part of their diet.

The Nez Percé, Spokane, Yakama, Cayuse, Okanogan, Walla Walla, and Colville tribes lived east of the Cascades. These eastern groups hunted deer, elk, bear, and small game. In the winter, they built large pithouses deep in the ground. The pithouses protected them from the cold and the wind.

". . . I assended a high [cliff] ... from this place I [discovered] a high mountain of [immense height] covered with snow, this must be one of the mountains laid down by Vancouver, as seen from the mouth of the Columbia River . . ."

—William Clark, October 19, 1805

Explorers

The first explorers came to Washington in the late 1700s. Two Spanish explorers landed near Point Grenville on the Columbia River in 1775. Bruno Heceta and Juan Francisco de la Bodega y Quadra were the first Europeans to land on Washington soil.

In 1778, Captain James Cook was the first British explorer to reach Washington. His reports of furbearing animals attracted many fur traders to the region.

Other explorers came to the region a few years later. In 1792, British Captain George Vancouver completed a detailed report of the Washington coast. He named many Washington landmarks, including Mount Rainier and Mount Baker. The same year, American Captain Robert Gray discovered the Columbia River. He named the river after his ship.

In 1804, Meriwether Lewis and William Clark led a group of about 30 explorers across the west. In 1805, they crossed the Rocky Mountains. They followed the Columbia River to the Pacific Ocean and mapped the area.

Founded in 1811, Fort Okanogan was the first U.S. settlement in Washington. It was located where the Okanogan and Columbia Rivers meet.

First Settlements

During the early 1800s, British and American fur traders operated in the region. They traded with American Indians for beaver pelts. In 1811, fur trader John Jacob Astor founded Fort Okanogan, the first U.S. settlement in Washington.

In 1825, the British Hudson's Bay Company built Fort Vancouver on the Columbia River. John McLoughlin was a successful trader who helped develop Fort Vancouver.

Great Britain and the United States both wanted control of areas north of the Columbia River. In 1846, the two countries agreed on the current border between Washington and Canada.

Settlement and a New Territory

In the 1830s, missionaries came to try to convert the Indians to Christianity. Marcus and Narcissa Whitman were missionaries

near the town of Walla Walla. A group of Cayuse Indians there became angry after a white man in California killed a Cayuse boy who had traveled there. They were also upset because measles, a disease brought by Europeans, was killing many people in the tribe. In 1847, the Cayuse killed the Whitmans and 12 other people.

Settlers came to the Puget Sound area in the 1850s and founded Seattle. The town was named after Chief Seatlh of the Suquamish Indians. The settlers could not pronounce the Indian word "Seatlh," so the town became known as Seattle.

Seattle's position near Puget Sound drew many settlers in the late 1800s. This photograph of a drawing shows Seattle in 1874.

In 1853, Congress created the Washington Territory. The first territorial governor, Isaac Ingalls Stevens, signed treaties with several American Indian groups. Most of these agreements were unfair to the Indians. By 1855, Stevens had convinced many American Indians to live on small reservations in the territory.

The Northern Pacific Railroad brought many settlers to Washington.

In 1855, miners discovered gold in northeastern Washington. Many people rushed to the area. When gold seekers entered reservation areas, American Indians attacked them. The U.S. Army came to protect the gold seekers. From 1855 to 1859, American Indians and Washington settlers fought a series of battles. The tribes were defeated.

Territorial Settlement

Discoveries of gold in British Columbia in 1858 and Idaho in 1890 attracted miners. Miners coming through the Washington Territory often bought supplies in Walla Walla.

The settlers wanted a railroad to help their territory grow. A local railroad line went through Walla Walla in 1875. In 1883, the Northern Pacific Railroad connected the East Coast to Puget Sound. The new railroad brought thousands of farmers, loggers, and miners to the Washington Territory.

By the end of the 1800s, several industries were doing well in Washington. Cattle and sheep grazed on the plains of eastern Washington. Farmers planted crops in the fertile valley areas. Shipbuilding was common along the coasts.

Statehood and Success

On November 11, 1889, President Benjamin Harrison signed Washington into the Union. It was the 42nd state. The state's first governor was Elisha P. Ferry.

The state profited from the 1897–1898 Klondike gold rush in Alaska and Canada's Yukon Territory. Seattle became the main supply center for gold miners. Farmers in eastern Washington sold food to the miners. The new state celebrated its economic success at the Alaska-Yukon-Pacific Exposition of 1909. This world's fair was held in Seattle to promote the area and its trade with Alaska, Japan, and Canada.

World War I and the Great Depression

The United States entered World War I (1914–1918) in 1917. Washington provided forest products, farm goods, and ships for the war effort. The state's economy grew stronger.

During the Great Depression (1929–1939), the U.S. economy suffered. Businesses closed and many workers in Washington lost their jobs. President Franklin Roosevelt started programs to improve the economy. The Public Works Administration created jobs for unemployed workers in Washington and other areas.

Grand Coulee Dam

Farmland in central Washington receives little rain. To irrigate the area, engineers wanted to build a dam across the Columbia River. Beginning in 1933, construction of the Grand Coulee Dam provided thousands of jobs during the Great Depression. It was completed in 1942.

The Grand Coulee Dam is the largest concrete dam in North America. It is 550 feet (168 meters) high and almost 1 mile (1.6 kilometers) long. It helps to irrigate more than 500,000 acres (202,350 hectares) of farmland in the Columbia Plateau.

World War II

World War II (1939–1945) helped end the Great Depression. Washington workers built new factories to produce aircraft. Aircraft manufacturer Boeing produced B-17 and B-29 bombers. Other factories manufactured defense equipment for the military. The jobs attracted workers from other states and Washington's population grew quickly.

The United States fought Japan during the war. The U.S. government feared that Japanese Americans might spy for Japan. Japanese Americans living west of the Cascades were ordered to move. They were sent to camps in eastern Washington or Idaho until the end of the war.

During the war, the Manhattan Project was a secret plan to produce an atomic bomb. Hanford Engineer Works in eastern Washington was one of the project sites. Thousands of workers came to Hanford to design, build, and operate the world's first nuclear reactor.

In August 1945, U.S. President Harry Truman approved dropping the atomic bomb on Hiroshima, Japan. A few days later, the United States dropped a second bomb on Nagasaki. The bombs caused a great deal of damage and killed many people. Japan surrendered, bringing World War II to an end.

A Growing State

Washington's economy continued to grow after the war. Thousands of defense workers stayed in Washington after the war. Many people worked in the aluminum and aircraft industries. New dams on the Columbia River provided irrigation for farms in central Washington. Inland ports

People from all around the world visited the Century 21 World's Fair in Seattle in 1962.

developed on the Columbia River. Many products could be shipped on the rivers.

In 1962, Seattle hosted Century 21. This world's fair featured exhibits about the space age and helped promote tourism in the state. Today, tourists can visit the fairgrounds. They can see the 605-foot (184-meter) Space Needle observation tower that was built for the fair.

In the 1980s and 1990s, high-tech companies attracted many workers to the state. The growth also created pollution and traffic problems, especially in the Puget Sound area. Washington is working on ways to encourage economic growth while protecting the environment.

Recent Challenges

The state faces another challenge. The Hanford Site, home of the Manhattan Project during World War II, is damaging the environment. Poisonous chemicals used in the nuclear reactor have polluted the site. The Washington State Department of Ecology is working with federal groups to clean up the Hanford Site. The cost to clean up the site could be billions of dollars. It may take several decades to complete.

In 2001, a strong earthquake shook the Seattle area. Roads sank, windows shattered, debris fell from buildings, and people were without power. One person died. Damage to the city totaled $237 million.

Walls of houses were destroyed during an earthquake that hit the Seattle area in 2001.

Washington's state capitol in Olympia echoes the design of the U.S. Capitol in Washington, D.C.

Chapter 4

Government and Politics

Washington has not created a new constitution since it became a state in 1889. But state lawmakers have added more than 90 constitutional amendments. The state's voters approved all of these additions or changes to the constitution.

Power to the Voters

The constitution gives Washington voters the power to suggest new laws. This power, called initiative, requires a person to collect signatures on a petition. If a person collects enough signatures to support a law, that law will be put on a ballot for voters. In 1999, state voters passed Initiative 695. This initiative was a vote to replace the state's high motor

> *"We approach the enormous challenges before us, not because they're easy—they're not—but because they're right for our state. And they're right for future generations to come."*
>
> Governor Gary Locke, January 15, 2002

vehicle tax with a $30 fee for each vehicle. The law was passed.

Voters also have the power of referendum. This power allows them to reject existing laws by collecting signatures. People can then vote for or against an existing law.

Politics

Land use is an important political issue in Washington. The state's population is growing quickly. Rapid growth can cause pollution and traffic problems. In 1990, Washington's legislators passed the Growth Management Act. This act helps officials plan the growth of cities.

Washington's voters are evenly divided between Republicans and Democrats. City voters in western Washington usually support Democrats, while rural voters usually vote for Republicans. In presidential elections, Washington voters have supported a nearly equal number of Republican and Democratic candidates.

In 1996, Washingtonians elected Democrat Gary Locke as governor. He became the first Chinese-American governor of any state in the nation. In 2000, he was reelected to serve a second term.

Governor Gary Locke held up his daughter after hearing that he won reelection in 2000.

Branches of Government

Washington's governor leads the executive branch. The executive branch carries out the state's laws and decides how to spend the state's money. Voters elect all executive officials to serve four-year terms.

The legislative branch is the branch of the government that makes laws. It consists of a senate and a house of representatives. Washington has 49 members in the senate. Senators serve four-year terms. The 98 members in the house of representatives serve two-year terms.

The judicial branch applies the law through the court system. People who commit lesser crimes are tried in municipal or district courts. People accused of more serious crimes are tried in the superior courts. The superior courts hold jury trials. These courts also hear juvenile, property, and family cases.

A person can appeal a case through the court of appeals. People who lose there can take their cases to the state supreme court. The supreme court is the highest court in Washington. Nine justices serve on this court.

Washington's State Government

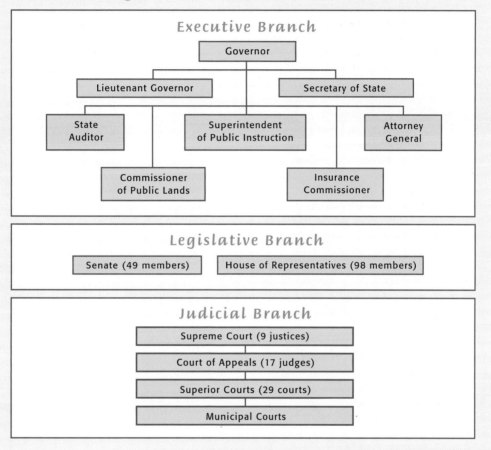

Executive Branch

- Governor
  - Lieutenant Governor
  - Secretary of State
  - State Auditor
  - Superintendent of Public Instruction
  - Attorney General
  - Commissioner of Public Lands
  - Insurance Commissioner

Legislative Branch

- Senate (49 members)
- House of Representatives (98 members)

Judicial Branch

- Supreme Court (9 justices)
- Court of Appeals (17 judges)
- Superior Courts (29 courts)
- Municipal Courts

Taxes

Unlike most states, Washington does not collect taxes on personal or business income. The state government's main source of income is a general sales tax on items that people buy. Taxes on property, gasoline, alcohol, and tobacco also bring money to the state.

Tourists enjoy hiking in Olympic National Park. Tourism is a large part of Washington's economy.

Chapter 5

Economy and Resources

Agriculture, forestry, and fishing were the main occupations of Washington's early European settlers. In the 1940s, manufacturing and service industries became an important part of Washington's economy. Today, Washington's economy relies on many industries.

Service Industries

Service industries employ more people than any other economic activity in the state. Service industries include tourism, health care, and education. Other examples are banking, real estate, retail sales, and government.

"But when the computer can satisfy curiosity and make learning fun, the possibilities get exciting. Kids . . . are proud to know more about something than an admired adult does."

Bill Gates, founder of Microsoft Corporation, 1995

Tourism has become a major source of income in Washington. Each year, visitors spend about $4.8 billion while visiting the state. Washington's national parks attract boaters, hikers, skiers, and nature lovers. Others enjoy visiting Seattle's many museums.

Manufacturing

The aerospace industry is the state's biggest manufacturing business. Aerospace companies produce airplanes, rocket parts, and equipment for space exploration. Boeing Company employs more people than any other company in the state.

Washington companies manufacture a variety of products. Microsoft Corporation is the largest computer software developer in the world. Its headquarters are in Redmond. Other products manufactured in Washington include computers, electronics, food, clothing, and industrial machinery. Many of Washington's manufacturing companies are located in cities along Puget Sound.

Bill Gates

William (Bill) Gates is the chairperson of Microsoft Corporation. It is a leader in computer software and services. He is the richest man in the world.

Gates began programming computers in Seattle when he was 13 years old. He and some friends wrote programs for companies. In exchange, they could use the company computers for free. At the time, computers were only used by businesses.

In 1973, Gates entered Harvard University. He later quit college to begin what is now Microsoft. He and his friend Paul Allen started this company in 1975. They began developing software for personal computers. They believed that someday computers would be very valuable in offices and homes. Today, Microsoft employs more than 50,000 people in 78 countries and regions.

Gates and his wife started a program called the Bill and Melinda Gates Foundation. They have given more than $24 billion to the foundation. One program the foundation supports brings computers and Internet access to low-income families.

Washington is a leading shipbuilding center. The Puget Sound Naval Shipyard is in Bremerton. It is the largest shipyard on the Pacific Northwest coast. Seattle, Tacoma, Everett, and Bellingham also have companies that build and repair ships.

Trees are one of Washington's natural resources. The state ranks second in the nation for producing lumber.

Washington produces about one-fourth of the nation's aluminum. This soft metal is refined from bauxite ore. Washington imports most of its bauxite from other countries. Aluminum is used to make soda cans, electrical equipment, vehicles, and kitchen products.

Forestry and Fishing

Washington ranks second among the states in producing lumber. The state's trees are used to make lumber, paper, and other wood products. The government and private companies work to maintain Washington's valuable lumber resources. They plant new trees in harvested forest areas.

Puget Sound and the Pacific Ocean provide opportunities for fishing industries. The state is one of the nation's leading producers of salmon. Halibut, flounder, tuna, and cod are other fish caught. Fishers also harvest oysters, crab, and shrimp.

Agriculture

Grain is one of the state's leading crops. Wheat is grown in the Columbia Plateau area. Washington leads the nation in the production of hops, a grain used to make beer.

Washington's other crops are varied. The state leads the nation in production of spearmint oil, lentils, and dry peas. It ranks second to Idaho in growing potatoes. The state is one of the world's chief producers of iris, tulip, and daffodil bulbs.

Farmers grow fruit in central Washington's irrigated valleys. Washington grows more apples than any other state.

The state produces more than half of the nation's apple crop. Famous types of Washington apples include Red Delicious, Golden Delicious, Granny Smith, and Fuji. Washington also leads the nation in producing Concord grapes, pears, and red raspberries.

Livestock also makes up part of Washington's agriculture. Milk and beef are the most important livestock products in Washington. Most of the dairy farms are west of the Cascades. Beef cattle graze in the eastern mountain regions. Farmers in the southeastern part of the state raise sheep.

Apples are a large crop for Washington. The state grows more than half the apples eaten in the United States each year.

Seattle's waterfront is famous for its restaurants and hotels.

Chapter 6

People and Culture

Washington is one of the 10 fastest-growing states in the nation. Between 1990 and 2000, Washington's population grew 21.1 percent. The state ranks 15th in population. Washington's scenic beauty, mild climate, and employment opportunities attract many new residents.

The People

More than 80 percent of the state's population lives in cities. The Puget Sound region is home to more than half of the population. The Seattle area grew very quickly during the 1990s. In 2000, the population of Seattle and its surrounding area was 3.6 million, an increase of 19.7 percent since 1990.

In the 1990s, cities in other regions of the state grew. Today, Spokane is the state's largest city east of the Cascades. Its population is 195,629.

Washington's population has a variety of ethnic backgrounds. Almost 79 percent of Washington's population is white. Most of these people have European backgrounds. Hispanic people make up 7.5 percent of the population. About 5.4 percent of the population is Asian. African Americans make up 3.1 percent of the population.

Washington has more than 90,000 American Indians who make up 1.4 percent of the population. The Yakama, Lummi, Quinault, Spokane, and Makah are some of the Indian groups living in Washington. Many of them live on the state's 27 reservations.

Festivals

Washingtonians find many ways to celebrate outdoors. The Ski to Sea festival is held in Bellingham every Memorial Day weekend. This 85-mile (137-kilometer) relay race starts at the top of Mount Baker and finishes in Bellingham Bay.

Washington's Ethnic Backgrounds

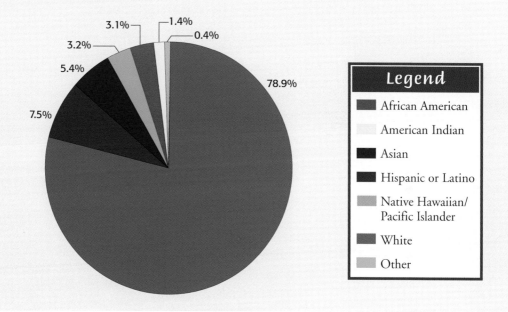

Legend
- African American
- American Indian
- Asian
- Hispanic or Latino
- Native Hawaiian/ Pacific Islander
- White
- Other

Cross-country skiers, runners, canoeists, bicyclists, and kayakers compete in the race. Salmon Days is an annual event in Issaquah. This festival, held each Labor Day, celebrates the return of the salmon. Visitors view exhibits, artwork, and visit the salmon hatchery.

Two of the largest festivals take place in Seattle. Bumbershoot is a huge arts festival held each summer. Artists, musicians, actors, and writers perform or display their work. Seattle's biggest festival of the year is Seafair, held in July and August. It features parades, boat races, and water carnivals.

The state's largest rodeo is held during Labor Day weekend in Ellensburg. Rodeo events include bull riding and calf roping. The Ellensburg Rodeo attracts many of the top bull riders and ropers in the country.

Bronc riding is a popular event at the Ellensburg Rodeo, held each September.

Chief Seattle Days is an annual festival in Suquamish each August. It celebrates the role American Indians played in the history of Washington state. It includes a memorial service at Chief Seattle's burial spot.

Museums and the Arts

Washington has several museums that cover the state's history. The Burke Museum of Natural History and Culture is at the University of Washington in Seattle. It has exhibits on natural history and the American Indians of the Pacific Northwest. The museum also has a skeleton of a 140-million-year-old allosaurus. The Museum of Flight in Seattle holds a collection of historical airplanes, including the first presidential jet.

Seattle is a center for music and theater in the state. The Seattle Symphony was formed in 1903. It has a national reputation. Seattle is also home to the Seattle Opera Association and the Seattle Repertory Theater.

Recreation and Sports

Washingtonians and tourists enjoy recreation in the state throughout the year. The state has three national parks and more than 125 state parks.

The Pacific Coast is a popular tourist area. State parks along the coastline provide opportunities for swimming, windsurfing, and scuba diving.

The state's rugged mountains attract mountain climbers and hikers. Mountain streams, lakes, and rivers offer fishing

and boating opportunities. Skiers enjoy resorts in the Mount Spokane and Cascade Range areas.

Washington has three pro sports teams. The Seattle Mariners baseball team plays in Safeco Field stadium. A new stadium for the Seattle Seahawks football team opened in 2002. The Seattle SuperSonics is Washington's pro basketball team.

Washington is a growing state with a strong economy. Citizens and tourists enjoy the beautiful scenery as well as recreational and employment opportunities.

Cross-country skiers compete in the Ski to Sea race. Skiing is popular as both a competitive and recreational sport.

Recipe: Granny Apple Crisp

Granny Smith apples grow in Washington. Many people use the green, tart apples in pies and desserts.

Ingredients

1½ cups (360 mL) oatmeal
2 cups (480 mL) brown sugar
3 teaspoons (15 mL) cinnamon
1 cup (240 mL) margarine
7 cups (1.7 liters) Granny Smith apples, peeled, cored, and cut into chunks
2 cups (480 mL) water
1½ cups (360 mL) sugar
2 teaspoons (10 mL) vanilla
4 tablespoons (60 mL) cornstarch

Equipment

large mixing bowl
mixing spoon
dry-ingredient measuring cups
measuring spoons
9- by 13-inch (23- by 33-centimeter) baking pan
nonstick cooking spray
medium saucepan
liquid-ingredient measuring cup
wooden spoon
oven mitts

What You Do

1. Preheat oven to 350°F (180°C).

2. In large mixing bowl, mix the oatmeal, brown sugar, cinnamon, and margarine until crumbly.

3. Grease baking pan with nonstick cooking spray. Spread half of crumb mixture in pan.

4. Cover crumb mixture evenly with apple chunks.

5. Combine the water, sugar, vanilla, and cornstarch in a saucepan.

6. Stir over medium heat until mixture makes a thick, clear syrup.

7. Pour hot syrup over apples.

8. Top with remaining crumb mixture.

9. Bake for one hour.

10. Remove from oven with oven mitts. Let cool before serving.

Makes about 20 servings

Washington's Flag and Seal

Washington's Flag

Washington adopted its state flag in 1923. The green background stands for Washington's evergreen forests. The state seal is in the center of the flag.

Washington's State Seal

Washington adopted its state seal in 1889, the year of statehood. Charles Talcott, a jeweler from Olympia, designed the original state seal. Talcott traced a circle around an ink bottle. Inside the circle, he traced a second one around a silver dollar. He wrote the words "The Seal of the State of Washington, 1889" between the two circles. In the center, he placed a picture of George Washington. In 1967, a portrait of George Washington by Gilbert Stuart became the official image on the center of the seal.

Almanac

Nickname: The Evergreen State

Population: 5,894,121 (U.S. Census 2000)

Population rank: 15th

Capital: Olympia

Largest cities: Seattle, Spokane, Tacoma, Vancouver, Bellevue

Agriculture

Agricultural products: Wheat, hops, apples, potatoes, lentils

Fishing: Salmon, cod, crab, flounder, herring, and oysters

Climate

Average winter temperature: 32.6 degrees Fahrenheit (0 degrees Celsius)

Average summer temperature: 63.5 degrees Fahrenheit (17.5 degrees Celsius)

Average annual precipitation: 37 inches (94 centimeters)

Geography

Area: 71,303 square miles (184,675 square kilometers)

Size rank: 18th

Highest point: Mount Rainier, 14,410 feet (4,392 meters) above sea level

Lowest point: Pacific Ocean, sea level

Coast rhododendron

Apple

Natural resources: Water, forests

Types of industry: Aerospace and computer software manufacturing, services, agriculture, forestry, shipbuilding

First state governor: Elisha P. Ferry, 1889–1893

Statehood: November 11, 1889; 42nd state

U.S. Representatives: 9

U.S. Senators: 2

U.S. electoral votes: 11

Counties: 39

Bird: Willow goldfinch

Fish: Steelhead trout

Flower: Coast rhododendron

Fossil: Columbian mammoth

Fruit: Apple

Gem: Petrified wood

Insect: Green darner dragonfly

Motto: "Al-ki"—an American Indian word meaning "by and by"

Ship: *President Washington*

Song: "Washington, My Home," by Helen Davis

Tree: Western hemlock

Timeline

State History

1500s
Many American Indian groups are living near the Cascades.

1775
Bruno Heceta and Juan Francisco de la Bodega y Quadra become the first known Europeans to land on Washington soil.

1792
Captain George Vancouver explores the Pacific Northwest.

1811
Fort Okanogan, the first United States settlement in Washington, is built.

1847
Cayuse Indians kill the missionaries at the Whitman Mission near Walla Walla.

1853
The U.S. Congress creates the Washington Territory.

1889
Washington becomes the 42nd state.

U.S. History

1620
The Pilgrims establish a colony in North America.

1775–1783
American colonists fight for their independence from Great Britain in the Revolutionary War.

1812–1814
The United States and Great Britain fight the War of 1812.

1861–1865
The Civil War is fought between Northern and Southern states.

1942
Grand Coulee Dam begins operation.

1996
Gary Locke is elected the nation's first Chinese-American governor.

1980
Mount St. Helens erupts.

2001
A strong earthquake shakes the Seattle area in February, causing more than $200 million in damage.

1962
Seattle hosts the World's Fair.

1929–1939
The U.S. economy suffers during the Great Depression.

1964
The U.S. Congress passes the Civil Rights Act, which makes discrimination illegal.

1939–1945
World War II is fought; the United States enters the war in 1941.

2001
On September 11, terrorists attack the World Trade Center and the Pentagon.

1914–1918
World War I is fought; the United States enters the war in 1917.

Words to Know

contaminated (kuhn-TAM-uh-nay-tid)—dirty or unfit for use

endangered (en-DAYN-jurd)—at risk of dying out

erupt (e-RUHPT)—to burst suddenly

initiative (e-NISH-uh-tiv)—the power to put laws on a ballot by petition

irrigate (IHR-uh-gayt)—to bring water to fields and crops

measles (MEE-zulz)—an infectious disease caused by a virus; measles causes a rash and fever.

pelt (PELT)—an animal's skin with the hair or fur still on it

peninsula (puh-NIN-suh-luh)—a piece of land attached to a larger land mass and surrounded by water on three sides

pollution (puh-LOO-shuhn)—harmful materials that damage the environment

reservation (rez-ur-VAY-shuhn)—land set aside for American Indians

sound (SOUND)—a long, narrow area of water between two other bodies of water or between the mainland and an island

temperate (TEM-pur-it)—having a mild climate

To Learn More

Bial, Raymond. *The Nez Perce.* Lifeways. New York: Marshall Cavendish, 2002.

Blashfield, Jean F. *Washington.* America the Beautiful. New York: Children's Press, 2001.

Bursell, Susan. *The Lewis and Clark Expedition.* Let Freedom Ring. Mankato, Minn.: Bridgestone Books, 2002.

Stefoff, Rebecca. *Washington.* Celebrate the States. New York: Benchmark Books, 1999.

Internet Sites

Do you want to find out more about Washington?
Let FactHound, our fact-finding hound dog, do the research for you.

Here's how:
1) Visit ***http://www.facthound.com***
2) Type in the Book ID number:
   0736822038
3) Click on **FETCH IT**.

FactHound will fetch Internet sites picked by our editors just for you!

Places to Write and Visit

Mount St. Helens National Volcanic Monument
Monument Headquarters
42218 NE Yale Bridge Road
Amboy, WA 98601

Office of the Governor
P.O. Box 40002
Olympia, WA 98504-0002

Olympic National Park
600 East Park Avenue
Port Angeles, WA 98362-6798

Washington State Historical Society
1911 Pacific Avenue
Tacoma, WA 98402

Washington State Tourism
Office of Trade and Economic Development
Raad Building
128 10th Avenue SW
P.O. Box 42525
Olympia, WA 98504-2525